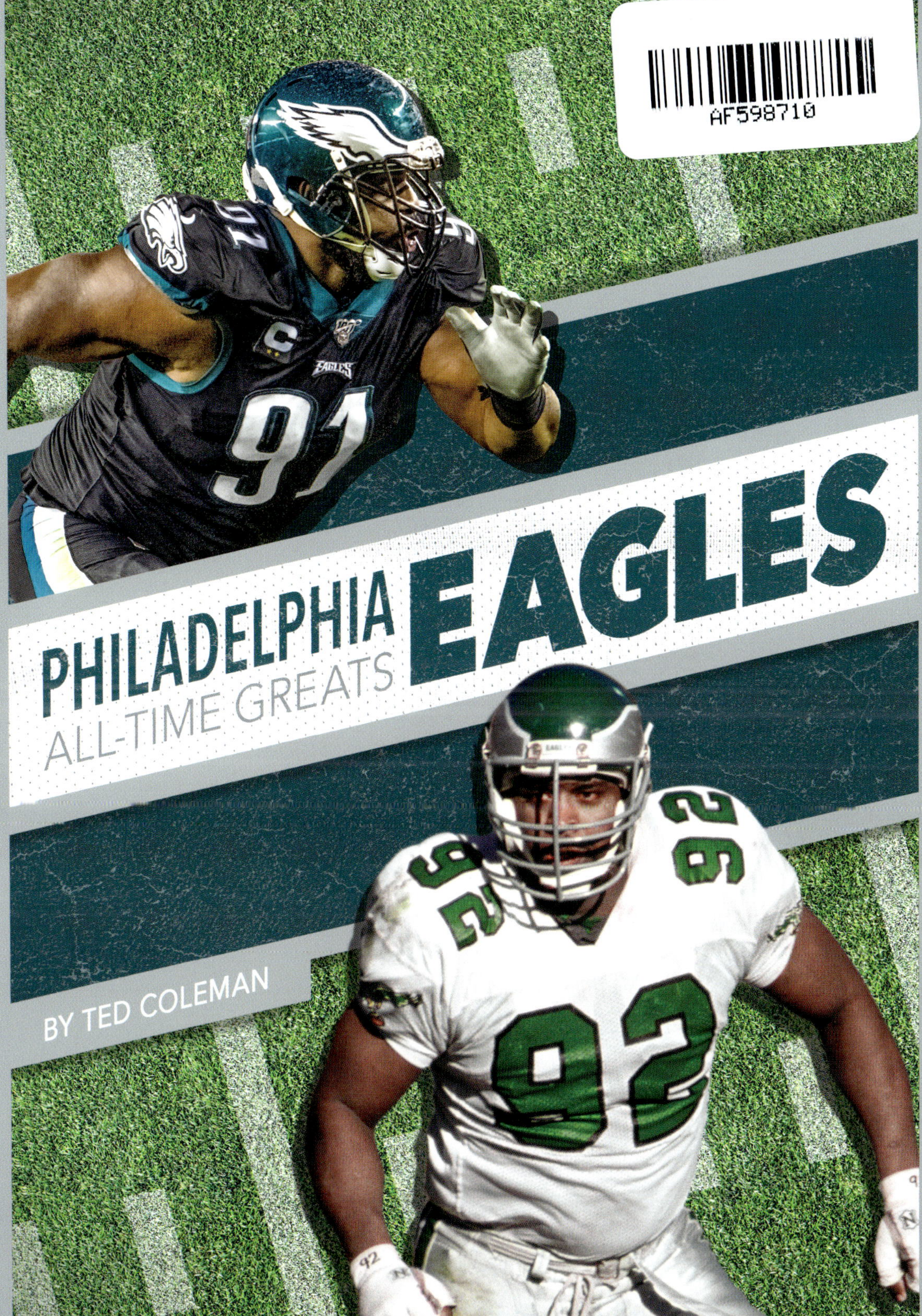
AF598710
PHILADELPHIA
EAGLES
ALL-TIME GREATS
BY TED COLEMAN

Book design by Jake Slavik
Cover design by Jake Slavik

Photographs ©: Al Tielemans/AP Images, cover (top), 1 (top); David Durochik/AP Images, cover (bottom), 1 (bottom), 12; AP Images, 4; Pro Football Hall of Fame/AP Images, 7; Sam Myers/AP Images, 8; Vernon J. Biever/AP Images, 10; Al Messerschmidt/AP Images, 13; Allen Kee/AP Images, 15; Dave Martin/AP Images, 16; Mel Evans/AP Images, 18; Chris Szagola/AP Images, 21

Press Box Books, an imprint of Press Room Editions.

ISBN
978-1-63494-363-5 (library bound)
978-1-63494-380-2 (paperback)
978-1-63494-413-7 (epub)
978-1-63494-397-0 (hosted ebook)

Library of Congress Control Number: 2020952631

Distributed by North Star Editions, Inc.
2297 Waters Drive
Mendota Heights, MN 55120
www.northstareditions.com

Printed in the United States of America
082021

ABOUT THE AUTHOR

Ted Coleman is a sportswriter who lives in Louisville, Kentucky, with his trusty Affenpinscher, Chloe.

TABLE OF CONTENTS

VAN BUREN
15

CHAPTER 1

EAGLES TAKE FLIGHT

The first championship for the Philadelphia Eagles came in 1948. Running back **Steve Van Buren** was the team's star. Van Buren was known as the "Moving Van." He wasn't flashy. He was simply a hard runner who kept the ball moving. When Van Buren retired after the 1951 season, he had the most rushing yards in National Football League (NFL) history.

The Eagles repeated as NFL champs in 1949. Tight end **Pete Pihos** helped lead the way. In those days, most tight ends were not good receivers. But Pihos was one of the best.

In nine seasons, he made six Pro Bowls. He also led the NFL in catches three times.

Chuck Bednarik almost never left the field. He missed only three games in 14 years. And he did that while playing both offense and defense. In the 1960 NFL title game, Bednarik played 58 of the game's 60 minutes. On offense, Bednarik played center. On defense, he was a bone-crushing tackler. Bednarik was the NFL's last two-way star.

Quarterback **Norm Van Brocklin** had planned to retire after the 1957 season. But he changed his mind, and he was traded

BERT BELL

Bert Bell once said all he ever wanted was to be a football man. After founding the Eagles in 1933, Bell went on to become the team's coach from 1936 to 1940. He then became commissioner of the NFL from 1946 until his death in 1959. Bell was inducted into the Pro Football Hall of Fame for his contributions to the sport.

from the Los Angeles Rams to the Eagles. Van Brocklin was a perfect fit for Philadelphia's high-flying offense. He made the Pro Bowl in all three of his seasons with the Eagles. In 1960, he was also the league's Most Valuable Player (MVP). Better yet, he led the Eagles to a championship.

McDONALD
25

VAN BROCKLIN
11

Wide receiver **Tommy McDonald** was Van Brocklin's favorite target. McDonald stood only 5-foot-9. But he had the speed to run away from defenders. In 1961, McDonald led NFL receivers with 13 touchdowns and 1,144 yards. His energy and enthusiasm also made him a popular teammate.

Pete Retzlaff didn't catch a single pass in his college career. But the Eagles made him into a receiver anyway. In 1958, Retzlaff hauled in 56 passes. That led the NFL. Retzlaff made the Pro Bowl five times. And he retired with the most receiving yards in Eagles history.

STAT SPOTLIGHT

YARDS PER CATCH

EAGLES TEAM RECORD

Tommy McDonald: 19.2

CARMICHAEL
17

CHAPTER 2

RETURN TO EXCELLENCE

Wide receiver **Harold Carmichael** came to Philadelphia in 1971. Unfortunately for Eagles fans, the team was at a low point. Philadelphia hadn't been to the playoffs in more than a decade. Carmichael was a good player. But the team didn't have a star quarterback until **Ron Jaworski** joined the team in 1977. Jaworski and Carmichael led the Eagles to the Super Bowl in the 1980 season. Carmichael ended up with more receiving yards than any other Eagle. And Jaworski became the team's leader in career passing yards.

In 1986, **Randall Cunningham** took over at quarterback. He brought a new set of skills to the Eagles offense. Cunningham was an outstanding runner. He shattered the team record for rushing yards by a quarterback. But he

DICK VERMEIL

Dick Vermeil came to the Eagles in 1976. Previously, he had spent two years as a college coach. In the 1975 season, he led UCLA to an upset of No. 1 Ohio State in the Rose Bowl. After that, he rebuilt the Eagles. The team had only four wins in 1976. But by the 1980 season, they were in the Super Bowl.

could pass, too. One of his favorite targets was **Mike Quick**. In only 101 career games, Quick had the fourth-most receiving yards in Eagles history.

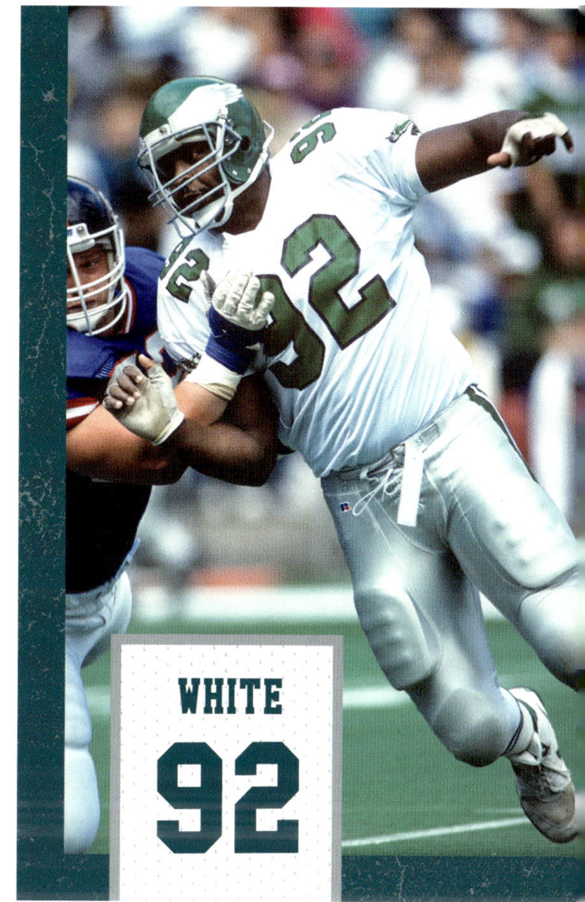

The Eagles were also known for their defense during this era. Defensive end **Reggie White** led the way. White entered the NFL in 1985. By 1986, he was in the Pro Bowl. And by

STAT SPOTLIGHT

CAREER SACKS

EAGLES TEAM RECORD

Reggie White: 124

1987, he was Defensive Player of the Year. He led the NFL with 21 sacks that year. In just eight seasons with the Eagles, the "Minister of Defense" became Philadelphia's all-time sack leader.

Defensive tackle **Jerome Brown** was on his way to stardom in 1992. He was coming off two straight Pro Bowl appearances. Sadly, he died in a car accident before the 1992 season began. The team retired his number before the first game of the season.

Cornerback **Eric Allen** could do more than cover receivers. In 1993, he led the NFL with four interceptions returned for touchdowns. His best was a 94-yard return for a game-winning score. By the time Allen left the Eagles, he was tied for the most picks in team history.

ALLEN
21

McNABB
5

CHAPTER 3

CHAMPS AGAIN

The Eagles slowly built a championship-level team in the late 1990s. Quarterback **Donovan McNabb** led the offense. He was a gifted runner, similar to Randall Cunningham. McNabb led the team to the Super Bowl in the 2004 season. And when he retired, he held every major team passing record.

STAT SPOTLIGHT

CAREER PASSING TOUCHDOWNS

EAGLES TEAM RECORD

Donovan McNabb: 216

Philadelphia's best player on defense was safety **Brian Dawkins**. He was a brutal hitter who played all over the field. Dawkins tied the team record of 34 interceptions.

The Eagles were blessed with two great running backs in a row. **Brian Westbrook** debuted in 2002. Just a third-round pick,

Westbrook became one of the best backs in team history. Westbrook was a great rusher and receiver. He retired as the team leader in total yards.

Westbrook's final year was 2009. That was the rookie year for **LeSean McCoy**. McCoy was a great receiver but an even better runner. He eventually became the Eagles' all-time leader in rushing yards. Known as "Shady," McCoy could quickly change direction to escape defenders.

The Eagles started a new era at quarterback when they drafted **Carson Wentz** in 2016.

DOUG PEDERSON

Andy Reid coached more games than anyone in Eagles history. He led the team to one Super Bowl, but the Eagles came up short in that game. Reid's former assistant **Doug Pederson** took over the head coaching job in 2016. And Pederson was able to achieve what Reid didn't. In the 2017 season, he won the first Super Bowl in team history.

In his first few seasons, Wentz played like an MVP. But he also got hurt a lot. After an injury in 2017, the team's Super Bowl hopes seemed to be over. But in came backup **Nick Foles**. Foles proved that he had what it took to be a champion. He led the Eagles to their first title since 1960.

No matter who was playing quarterback, tight end **Zach Ertz** was a top target. Ertz had great hands, and he became one of the best receivers in the game. In 2018, he racked up more than 1,000 receiving yards. He also caught 116 passes. That was a new NFL record for tight ends.

On defense, the Eagles were led by **Fletcher Cox**. Cox had an impressive combination of size, strength, and quickness. That helped him rack up plenty of sacks. In

fact, he made six straight Pro Bowls from 2015 to 2020. Cox showed Eagles fans that he was one of the team's all-time greats.

TIMELINE

1944
STEVE VAN BUREN
(1944–51)
PETE PIHOS
(1947–55)
1950
CHUCK BEDNARIK
(1949–62)
PETE RETZLAFF
(1956–66)
TOMMY McDONALD
(1957–63)
1960
NORM VAN BROCKLIN
(1958–60)
1970
HAROLD CARMICHAEL
(1971–83)
RON JAWORSKI
(1977–86)
1980
MIKE QUICK
(1982–90)
RANDALL CUNNINGHAM
(1985–95)
1990
JEROME BROWN
(1987–91)
REGGIE WHITE
(1985–92)
ERIC ALLEN
(1988–94)
BRIAN DAWKINS
(1996–2008)
2000
DONOVAN McNABB
(1999–2009)
BRIAN WESTBROOK
(2002–09)
2010
NICK FOLES
(2012–14, 2017–18)
LeSEAN McCOY
(2009–14)
ZACH ERTZ
(2013–)
FLETCHER COX
(2012–)
CARSON WENTZ
(2016–20)
2020

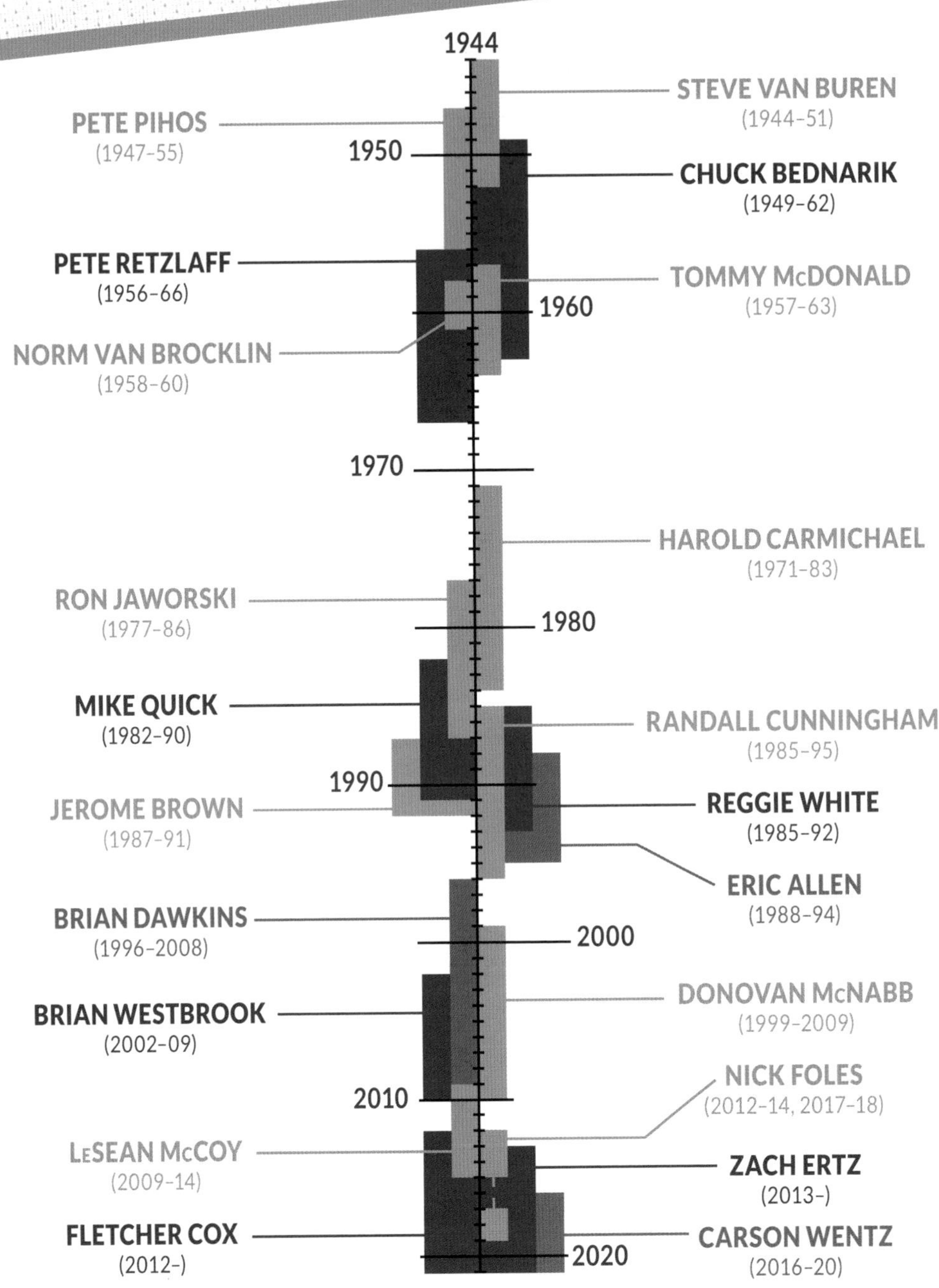

TEAM FACTS

PHILADELPHIA EAGLES

Founded: 1933

Other names: Phil-Pitt "Steagles" (1943)

NFL championships: 3 (1948, 1949, 1960)

Super Bowl titles: 1 (2017)*

Key coaches:

Greasy Neale (1941–50), 63–43–5,
2 NFL championships

Buck Shaw (1958–60), 19–16–1,
1 NFL championship

Andy Reid (1999–2012), 130–93–1

Doug Pederson (2016–2020), 42–37–1,
1 Super Bowl title

MORE INFORMATION

To learn more about the Philadelphia Eagles, go to **pressboxbooks.com/AllAccess**.

These links are routinely monitored and updated to provide the most current information available.

**1966 through 2020*

GLOSSARY

cornerback
A defensive player who covers wide receivers near the sidelines.

draft
An event that allows teams to choose new players coming into the league.

era
A period of time in history.

Pro Bowl
The NFL's all-star game, in which the league's best players compete.

sack
A tackle of the quarterback behind the line of scrimmage.

safety
A defensive player who covers wide receivers in the middle of the field.

INDEX